This igloo book belongs to:

....

igloobooks

Published in 2019
by Igloo Books Ltd
Cottage Farm
Sywell
NN6 0BJ
www.igloobooks.com

1119 001
2 4 6 8 10 9 7 5 3 1
ISBN 978-1-78905-683-9

Written by Melanie Joyce
Illustrated by Gail Yerrill

Printed and manufactured in China

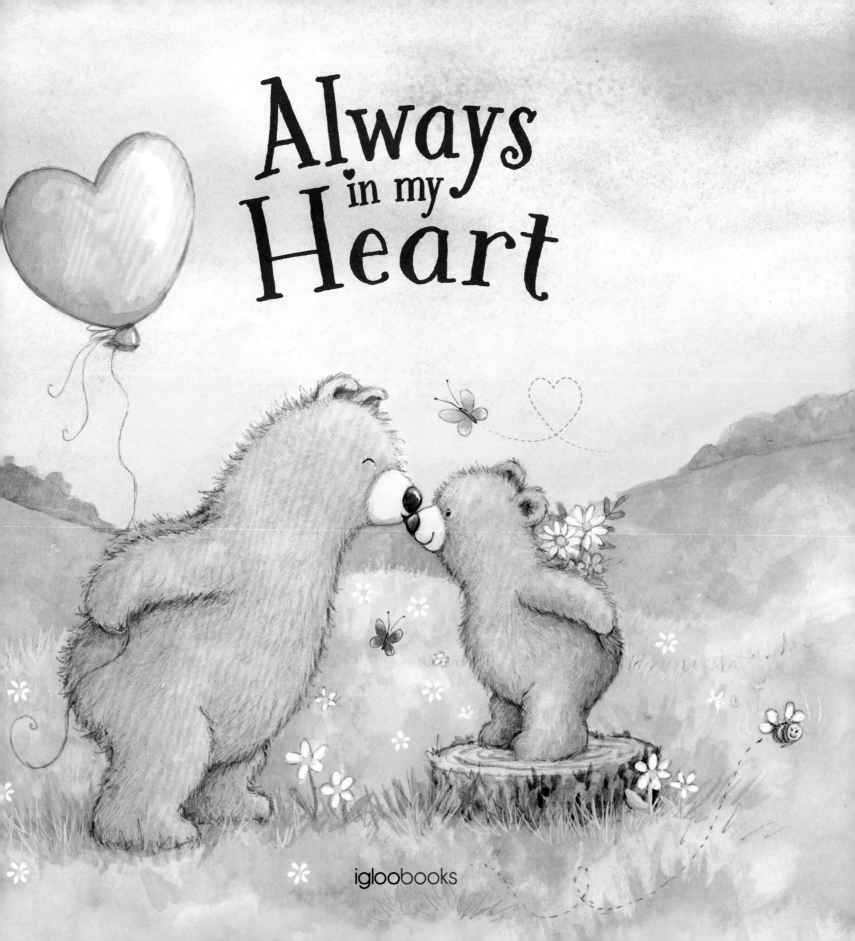

Always in my Heart

igloobooks

I love you so much and hardly know
where to start to tell you why you
are so special and always in my heart.

When I take you in my arms at the beginning
of the day, you smile sleepily at me.
"I love you, Mummy," you say.

You get so excited when you go outside and play.
"Catch me, Mummy!" you cry, as you
giggle and run away.

You search for me in the garden when we play hide-and-seek. You really make me laugh because you always giggle and peek.

You love to explore new places and look up at the sky. We lie in flower meadows and watch the clouds go by.

In the afternoon, when it's time for your nap, your little eyes go sleepy and you climb into my lap.

When you wake up, you are happy and play with all your toys. You think it's just so funny to make lots and lots of noise!

You've got the cutest little nose that wrinkles when you laugh. It does it when the bubbles burst in your splashy bath.

When it's time for bed you say, "Mummy, can we cuddle?" We settle down together and read stories as we snuggle.

You are always in my heart, because in your eyes I see all the love in the world looking back at me.